Advanc

Crystal Work

By Paul McCarthy

Copyright©2020 by Paul McCarthy

To contact the Author

You can contact the author by email at guidedbythelight@hotmail.com

Website: https://paulmccarthychannel.com/

The previous Books "Ascension, Spiritual Growth & Ascended Master", "Star Seeds, ET's & Star Beings", "Learn to Channel your Guides" and "Otherkin An introduction to Fairy, Elf & Angel Seeds" are available to purchase through Amazon.

Contents

Introduction

I have been attuning crystals with spiritual energies for the past fourteen years as part of my new age work with clients all over the world. Attuning crystals is also known as programming crystals. My students have often asked me how to attune crystals and so I hope that this book helps those who want to attune crystals correctly. Unfortunately, many people make mistakes when attuning crystals and so it is important to know how to do this correctly. In this book, I have explained why this happens and how to avoid making such mistakes.

Although I own many crystals, I exclusively use the clear quartz crystals for my work as they offer incredible advantages over the other crystals when they are attuned with energies. This book will explain why this is and how you too can successfully attune clear quartz crystals. This book does not look at crystals in general, only the clear quartz crystals and the advanced uses of these when we attune or program them with specific energies.

As a new age teacher, healer and channel, in my work I need something that can hold spiritual energies so that my students and clients can access these energies themselves. By attuning round quartz crystals, I am able to achieve this and to date I have distributed tens of thousands of these to my clients and students all around the world. At one stage I had bought all the medium sized quartz tumble stones crystals from the UK's two largest wholesale suppliers! They are extremely popular as they can hold literally any energy that I can imagine and someone else can easily access this energy when they hold the crystal. Although using crystals in this way is not a common approach, those who attend my workshops know that working that I will usually bring with me a large bag of attuned crystals. In one workshop in Vienna, I underestimated the number of crystals I needed and when I explained that some workshops participants might not get all of the crystals in the set, there was an actual stampede amongst the normally civilised participants to get to the crystals table where they could buy them!

The main benefit of attuning crystals is that you can attune any energy that you want and these can include: healing energies, star energies, meditation energies, the energies of guides, ascension or spiritual growth energies, activation energies and the energies of sacred sites. The energies can be general as in general healing energies or very specific as in the exact healing energy for migraines for example. Attuned crystals can hold subtle energies as in the energies of a flower or enormous energies like the energy of Andromeda Galaxy! Whatever you can imagine is possible. I once attuned the energy of a crystal to coffee and someone holding it reported they could taste coffee by holding it!

Another amazing fact about working with clear quartz crystals is that you cannot fail to notice the great intelligence that these crystals connects us to. This spiritual intelligence is very interactive and can fulfil requests. For example when using attuned crystals in workshops I often place a crystal on the floor and request it to increase/decrease the energies, stop / start the energies or to connect the group to something else that I want to work with. The crystal immediately responds to my request. Even more impressive than this is how I attune the crystal to select the correct energy for different clients. I call these galactic master crystals as for me I am working with the intelligence of the Galaxy itself. An example of this is my "Home" crystal where the crystal connects each star seed client to the star that they are connected to. I personally do not know this information and yet each person that holds the crystal is connected to the energy of the star they are linked to! This interactive intelligence that we connect to through working with attuned crystals is profound and we can benefit greatly from working with it.

I hope that my book will give you the inspiration and the tools to work with attuning clear quartz crystals too.

Paul McCarthy

Developing your Sensitivity to Energies

Before you start attuning crystals, it is important to sensitise yourself to energies so that you can feel the energies and be able to recognise them. It is possible to attune crystals without being able to sense the energies, however I do not recommend doing this as I find many people incorrectly believing that they have attuned crystals with energies when they have not and *they are not aware of this*. There are lots of ways mistakes that can be made and the only way of spotting if you have made one is to feel the energies after attuning a crystal in order to make sure that the attunement has been correctly performed. Some of these mistakes are listed below.

If you cannot sense energies, you can develop a sensitivity by working with energies. You can do this in a number of ways such as:

*Holding crystals (attuned or not) in your hands and sensing the energies.

*Receiving and giving healing.

*Performing any energy work or guide work whilst in meditation.

When you hold an attuned crystal, it is important to mentally acknowledge the crystal and say "hello" to it. This allows the crystal to engage with your own energies. This may sound strange, but I have seen many students holding a crystal and getting nowhere with it until I ask them to do this. Quartz crystals are not just objects as they connect us to a great intelligence which is undeniably spiritual in nature. This technique gives us a nudge to reach out to the energies of the crystal with our thoughts and our own energies.

When working with energy you will register it in your own way. Everyone experiences energies in different ways. Some of these experiences include:

*Feeling activity around your body and in your aura.

*Feeling activity in your body.

*Sensing a change of mood or emotional state.

*Seeing images or colours in your mind's eye or imagination.

*Having spiritual experiences which can be experienced as a sense of bliss, extasy or pure expanded awareness.

The trick is to sense how the energy is making YOU feel different from before. That difference can be described as the function of the energy. Your body, aura and emotions are telling you what the energy is doing to you or in other words they are describing the function or effect of the energy of the crystal.

A lot of people are initially cannot sense energies but can develop a sensitivity. Often women are initially more sensitive to energies than men, but I know some men who have worked hard to achieve a great sensitivity and this has opened doors for them. I remember one young man who came to my workshops in Copenhagen initially could not feel anything at all. After attending a number of my workshops, he can now sense the

most subtle of energies and he uses his
sensitivity by sharing a new found skill working
with spiritual art.

*The more we work with energies the more
sensitive we become to spiritual energies in
general.*

How to attune quartz crystals

I only use round clear quartz crystals as they hold energy well and they are known to be the best choice from all the crystals for this function. I have tried pointed crystals and I cannot get the same effect. Hopefully, you have a round shaped clear quartz crystal and now just follow these steps:

1. Using your focused will, invoke the energy that you want to attune the crystal with.
2. Wait until you feel this energy around you in whatever ways you register energies.
3. Hold the crystal in either hand.
4. Now imagine little lines of energy emerging from the crystal and connecting to the energy you have invoked.
5. Wait a few seconds for this to complete and try to notice how the crystal now radiates out the energy.
6. Please take a break from this and come back to the crystal and check

that it holds the energy that you
wanted.

Notes

To check the crystal is holding the new energy
correctly, you can put down the crystal down
and take a break in order to let the energy from
the attunement dissipate. Now as you check the
crystal you are fresh and disconnected from the
attunement and are able to simply observe the
energy in the crystal.

Be like a robot!

The key to attuning crystals correctly is to act
like a robot and to be emotionless when we
attune crystals. We have to focus solely on the
energy we want to be held by the crystal. Here is
an example of how many people make mistakes
with this process. At a workshop, a participant
presented me with a crystal she had attuned and
wanted me to check. She had attempted to
attune the crystal to the energies of Mother
Mary so that she could connect to her more
easily. When I sensed the energies of her
crystal, I did not feel the energies of Mother

Mary but instead I sensed her love of Mother Mary. She had mistakenly attuned the crystal with her emotions rather than the energy of this guide. When she performed the attunement of the crystal she was clearly exploding with her love of Mother Mary which is lovely but it does not work for attuning crystals. We have to be emotionless in order to avoid this as the crystal will attune itself to whatever you are beaming at it.

It was interesting when my translator at my Japanese workshop told me that my approach was identical to that of the Dr Emoto who was famous for attuning water and then photographing the magnified crystalline shapes of the water molecules. She had worked as his translator too when he toured the world and so had heard both of us saying the same thing even though we had never met or worked together.

Which hand to use?

There are different opinions about which hand needs to be used to hold the crystal when we attune it. In my experience it does not matter which hand you use. I know this because I can attune a crystal remotely without even touching it. Often in workshops I place a crystal in the centre of the room without holding it and I attune it from a distance. Personally, I normally hold the crystal in my left hand and place my right hand over this. I only do it this way as it focuses my intention and not because this is the correct way to do this.

The energy seems to fade with my attunement crystal

Attuned crystals will hold the energy until the end of time. The only way to remove this energy is to attune it to another energy. I often wonder what people might think in the future if they discover the many crystals I have attuned as the energies will still be there!

But it is true that for some people who use attuned crystals, that it can feel to them that over time the energies feel less strong. The reason for this is that they become accustomed to the energies and the contrast between the effect of the energy on them and how they normally feel become less noticeable. If this happens to you, you can simply ask the crystal to make the energy stronger or present it to you in new ways. Please read my notes on the "intelligence" of crystals.

Do I need to cleanse the crystal?

It is a popular idea that crystals "pick up" people's energies. This is why it is a common recommendation that you cleanse crystals before you use them. In all the years of working with tens of thousands of crystals, I can tell you that I have never found a single crystal that holds a person's energy. So why is this idea so popular? I think that some people do experience other people's energies when they hold a new crystal, but it is not for the reason they believe.

Crystals act as portals and I have a chapter in this book explaining this. Briefly a portal is anything that connects you to something else. Quartz crystals can connect you to any being or energy that you can think of. This portal activity is triggered by thoughts as crystals respond to your thoughts and will treat them as instructions. So if a person is holding a crystal and thinking about the people who have held that crystal recently, then the crystal will take it as an instruction to connect that person to the people who have held it and hence they feel their energies. So, we have to understand how crystals really work so that we know how to use them and how not to use them.

As such there is no reason to cleanse crystals when you first receive them. If you are attuning a crystal to a new energy, then the new attunement will remove whatever energy was attuned before.

Other methods to attune crystals

I have seen people try and use other methods to attune crystals and I really do not see these working. I once examined some crystals attuned with the vibrations from a large crystal bowl. The crystals had no attuned energies at all and so I know this does not work. Another example is when people place crystals next to other crystals and then assume that the energy will transfer across the crystals as part of an osmosis type effect. Again, I have seen no evidence that this works.

The reality is that attuning crystals works when we intend this to happen and place a focus on this. We facilitate this new energy and when we move away from this approach and leave the process to other factors, it no longer works.

I remember once, a young man in my Oslo workshop approached me with a manufactured example of a mass-produced spiritual symbol he had ordered. When I examined the device, I could not feel any energies. It was unfortunate as he had spent some money on producing these and it had not worked. When we move away from attuning crystals (or other things) personally using our spiritual and energetic gifts, we lose the ability to program energy into the object we are working with. This is why mass-produced products often do not work in terms of carrying energies.

It is possible to attune as many crystals as you can hold all in one go. Sometimes I attune up to twenty crystals all with the same energy by piling them up in my hand.

Symbols

Obviously, some spiritual symbols carry energies in the same way as attuned crystals. Universal symbols often carry energies, however it is not true to think that it is the symbol only that has the power to hold the energy. You can work with symbols and even create some yourself. However, the same truths we know about attuning crystals applies to symbols. We have the power to choose and attune the energy in the symbol. I have demonstrated this in workshops by drawing a symbol on paper. I then folded the paper and passed it around my workshop participants and asked them to feel the energy. They agreed it was a high energy and they expected to see a sophisticated spiritual symbol. I then revealed the symbol which was a cartoon smiley face! The point of the exercise is that it is not necessary to have an amazing spiritual symbol with sacred geometry and all the bells and whistles. Attuning the energy can be achieved by our intention and the focused act of attuning the energy only.

Which Energies and Materials to use

The main point of attuning crystals is to hold an energy of your choice in order to benefit from that energy when you hold it. As I have mentioned before, you can literally choose any energy that you want. If the sky is the limit, then what are you going to choose? You can start with the energies that you know and want. I hope that from the examples below you will see some ideas that you can use or inspire you to come up with other ideas.

To start with we can identify some of the general areas of crystal work as below:

- Healing Energies
- Psychic and Channeling Energies
- Spiritual Growth / Ascension Energies
- Wellbeing Energies
- Manifestation Energies
- Energetic Work
- Meditation Work

Healing Energies Examples

*Healing Blocks (letting go of emotion and energetic links to issues or experiences from the past.)

*Balancing Energies and Chakras

*Illness specific energies-These are the precise healing energies that are needed to work in holistic ways to help with specific conditions such as Fibromyalgia, Colitis, M.E., Migraines, IBS, Panic Attacks, Thyroid, Rheumatoid Arthritis, Depression (spiritual and not clinical), Multiple Sclerosis, Allergies, Addictions and Inflammation.

Please be careful with this as it is illegal to advertise that you can heal or cure certain illnesses such as cancer.

Psychic and Channeling Energies Examples

*Raising vibration needed for channeling

*Activation of the third eye

Spiritual Growth / Ascension Energies Examples

*Impulse to ascend

*Transcendence

*Acceptance

*Divine Realisation

*Divine Surrender

Well Being Energies Examples
*De-Stress
*Creativity
*Peace

Manifestation Energies Examples
*General Manifestation Energies
*Manifestation - Romance
*Manifestation- Money

Energetic Work Examples
*Energy Clearance
*Energy Flow
*Energy Integration
*Soul Healing

Meditation Work Examples
*Alpha brain wave state
*Theta brain wave state

What can we attune?

It is possible to attune energies using other materials instead of crystals. Here is an examination of some other choices:

Water – Water can hold energies, at least for a period. There is a common psychic development exercise where individuals imprint their energies on a bowl of water and someone else then reads the energy. Of course, quartz crystals are linked to water in the sense that they grow from silica-rich water. In my opinion water is not a good choice to hold energies as they tend to dissipate in water in a short period of time.

Stone – All stones can hold energies. Indeed, if you have ever visited an ancient temple or stone circle you can feel the energies that they hold. Of course, with some temples and stone circles such as Stonehenge there are additional factors responsible for shaping the energies. You can even feel the energies in some stone statues in museums. In the British Museum there is a row of statues of the Egyptian Goddess Sekhmet and one of which holds some great energies. Clearly this specific statute has been attuned to energies and the others are just stone statues. I have heard stories of the Master Jesus attuning pebbles, but I have no other information about this. In my opinion attuning stones is not the best choice as the results of the energies are less effective than with other choices such as crystals. The energies with stone are felt more at a physical level and seem to be capped in the sense that they do not expand to all the levels of non-physical realities.

Oil – Oils such as rape seed oil can hold energy well. Although I do not use this method, I have inspected vials of oil attuned to specific energies and they did work well. The problem with this method is that you have to buy and store these vials and there is of course always a danger of them being broken and of them leaking.

Paper – It is possible to attune paper with energies. Spiritual authors often do this unwittingly in the sense that their writing is imbued with their own energies but not specific energies. If you want to attune a single piece of paper, you can write or draw anything you want as long as you focus on the energy you want to be attuned. However, if you publish a book or arrange for a printer to mass produce this, I wonder if this will work? As mentioned previously the more we let go of the process of production the more likely it is to fail and not hold the energies.

Metal – It is possible to attune metals. I have tried this, but I have to say the results are weird. Although there is a semblance of the intended energy, it feels incomplete and awkward. I suppose metals are less natural the above choices and maybe this is why it does not seem to work as well.

Crystal – In my opinion clear quartz crystals are the best choice for attuning energies. They hold the energies well and over all levels that we can perceive them unlike other choices. The cost of normal clear quartz tumblestones is low and they can be transported very well. Quartz crystals will hold the energies forever and will not lose the energies unless the crystal is deliberately re- attuned to another energy.

We must be responsible about what choices of energy we attune. I would not advise attuning crystals to energies that take away someone's else's free will or that brings them negativity. This is a universal principle and anyone ignoring this will could create problems for themselves. This brings up the long standing and traditional definition of white and black magic. White magic is where we use our gifts to try and help others and black magic is where we use them for selfish purposes. I do not think using energies to enhance our ability to attract money is black magic as we live in a world where everything revolves around money and we all need money even if it is to just to support our spiritual work. However, such goals as to gain power for powers sake or to try and manipulate people's thoughts and emotions for our own benefit probably do count as black magic. Ultimately you must decide what is the right use of energies and crystals.

Using Crystals as Portals

Quartz crystals can be attuned to act as a portal. This means the crystal can connect us to the energies of whatever you seek to connect to, even across all time and space. Here are some examples of this in practice:

I have attuned individual quartz crystals to other places or realms such as:

Stars and Star beings from the stars Sirius, Orion, Pleaides, Arcturus and Vega.

Places and periods of time on earth such Atlantis and Lemuria.

Other realms such as the Fairy, Elf or Angelic realms.

Sacred sites such as Stonehenge, Avebury, Glastonbury, Egyptian Temples such the Sphinx and the great pyramids and others like Machu Pichu.

These work by connecting you to the energies of these specific places or realms. By holding the crystal, you can sense the energies of the specific place that the crystal has been attuned to. These energies can connect your awareness to that place. This means you can experience it, possibly see it and explore it in whatever you can sense. You can also use these crystals to connect to beings from that place. In some ways it is almost as if you are there. These portals connect you to these places and then it is for you to decide what you would like to see and experience.

I have also created sets of attuned crystals that I call "Room" crystals which we use in any room we want to create a portal and connect us to the energies of another place. Examples of this are the Sirian Temples or the Angelic Realms. Here I use four attuned crystals which can be placed in the corners of the room to define the area and a master crystal that controls the energies. These infuse the room with the energies and connection to a places or realm. This great for creating whatever energetic atmosphere you want. For example, the energy of peace in a meditation room or yoga room and creative energies in a room where you paint, write or create music. You could create a temple room using your favourite energy and connection such as Sirius, Pleiades, Arcturus or the Angelic, Fairy or Elf realms.

Other examples are my Ashtar and Arcturus Light Pads. These connect the user to the energies of the light ship connected to these star beings. Each pad contains six individual crystals that connect the user to different sections of the light ships such as the healing room.

These are my examples and I am sure you can think of other ways to use these quartz portals.

I once watched an episode of Ancient Aliens where it was suggested that sightings of the Loch Ness Monster were due to the large content of quartz in the rocks around Loch Ness. It was suggested that the quartz in the rocks acts as a portal and occasionally connects onlookers to the past when these creatures existed in the loch. The suggestion is that these are paranormal experiences prompted by the effect of quartz crystals whereby people are seeing visions of the past and mistakenly thinking that it is happening in the current time. I am not a geologist and so I cannot say that this is true, however it makes sense to me as I know the potential of quartz to act as a portal. This theory explains why this creature cannot be found in the Loch and yet there are many sightings of it.

How do you use quartz crystals to act as a portal?

I would suggest that you attune a quartz crystal to the specific energy of a place or realm and use the crystal in your meditations to connect to that place. This method ensures that you connect to the correct energy and place and that the connection is maintained for as long as you need it to be. It is possible to work with quartz crystals that have not been attuned and use them to connect you to other energies, beings or places. Here you are relying on the portal like effect of quartz crystals to connect you to whatever you have in your mind. If you are wanting to do this, you have to be very focused on what you are thinking of, as quartz will connect you to whatever you are thinking about or feeling emotionally. Please see my previous writing about cleansing crystals. In addition, if you work with crystals that have not been attuned, then you have to realise that as your thoughts wander off to other things, the portal like connection will be diminished or lost.

Etheric Crystals

These are the counterparts to crystals in the physical universe that exist in the etheric realms. They are more like energy than physical objects. Seen in psychic visions they appear as almost watery pools of energy that can move and be positioned where desired. They can be attuned with energy that can help us. Etheric crystals can be created by thought alone and also by guides. Because you can place an etheric crystal in specific locations in your energy fields, this type of work lends itself to specific tasks. An example of the use of etheric crystals might be to place an etheric crystal near the heart centre to provide healing energy for the heater centre. They do not tend to last forever as in common with all things in the etheric realms, the form of etheric crystals tends to be more fluid and malleable compared to the physical nature of crystals in the physical universe.

Guides work a lot with etheric crystals. If you work with guides in the areas of healing and activation work, then etheric crystals will probably have been used by guides when they work with your energies even if you are unaware of this. An example of this is when I take my students on a guided meditation around the Ashtar Light Ship. On arrival there, an Ashtar guide places an etheric crystal above the left shoulder of all the visitors which raises their energies to match those of the ship. This is deactivated when they leave.

Using etheric crystals is not necessarily a better way to use energies compared to working with attuned physical crystals as you can benefit from the same energies using either method. In my own opinion as etheric crystals are not permanent and can fade away in a short period of time, physical crystals have the advantage. Only the energies within attuned physical crystals last for considerable periods of time.

Attuned Crystals for clients

If you can attune crystals and check your work, it may be that you want to share your gifts and the energies that you are working with by attuning crystals for clients. It is a great way to encourage others to work with healing and spiritual energies. It is a wonderful way to enjoy energies as people love physical things and the crystal itself is attractive and invites people to hold it and connect to the energies. In addition, the following benefits exist:

If you are working with clients and spiritual energies:

Students tend to lack the confidence needed and indeed the ability to connect to energies directly. They appreciate the attuned crystals as they feel the "work" is being done for them and they can trust them, relax and enjoy the benefits.

Attuned crystals hold their energies forever unless they are re-attuned. This means if students need an energy connection that lasts for longer periods of time then attuned crystal can give them this. If a person connects directly with an energy without using attuned crystals, then the session will only last as long as they can maintain a strong focus on it. For most people this can be only for a few minutes.

If you are sharing your attuned quartz crystals with others, please remember to help them to sense the energies using my suggestion from a previous chapter which is below:

When you hold an attuned crystal, it is important to mentally acknowledge the crystal and say "hello" to it. This allows the crystal to engage with your own energies. This may sound strange, but I have seen many students holding a crystal and getting nowhere with it until they do this. Quartz crystals are not just objects and they connect us to a great intelligence which is undeniably spiritual in nature. This technique gives us a nudge to reach out to the energies of the crystal with our own thoughts and energies.

What next?

Please try and attune crystals yourself and make sure to check your work afterwards. Please be inspired to try new energies and ideas. I am sure that there are many possibilities that we have not yet thought of!

I still work with my attuned crystals in my workshops and you are welcome to attend these to use the many attuned crystals I work with which may not be mentioned in this book. In addition, I have a newsletter that highlights new products and services including new attuned crystal sets. Please visit my website below if you want to sign up for this and receive these by email.

You can contact me using the contact information below.

Paul's website -
https://paulmccarthychannel.com/

Paul's email – guidedbythelight@hotmail.com

AND PLEASE …

If you liked this book and want to see more of my writing in the future, I'd really appreciate a review on Amazon. The number of reviews a book receives has a direct impact on how it sells, so just by leaving a review, no matter how short, helps make it possible for me to continue to do what I do.

Printed in Great Britain
by Amazon

63477075R10023